FULLY ADVENTUROUS

Trailblazing Voyages from History

Stories to Take Your Breath Away

Some people think history is dead and buried. It happened so long ago, it must be dead dull, right? Wrong! Just because the past is long gone, that doesn't mean it has to be forgotten. Historical stories can live on – forever!

So where can you find these stories? In books just like this one, written by modern authors who are fully interested in the past. These authors look at different sources of information like old letters, paintings and maps. Then, bit by bit, they piece together stories that breathe life back into the past and take your breath away.

Contents

You probably know a lot about the world. Perhaps you can even name all the oceans and continents on a map. But have you ever wondered who first found out what the world looked like? The answer: a lot of fully adventurous guys! They boldly sailed into the unknown from their homes in Europe, blazed a trail around the world, then left us with the stories of their adventures. Want to know more? Keep reading!

Chapter 1

What's Over the Horizon? **4**

Fearless European sailors braved the dangerous seas to discover foreign lands. But why?

Chapter 2

Vessels of the Vikings **9**

From the 8th century to the 11th, northern European sailors struck fear wherever they went.

Chapter 3

Spice Boys! **12**

Portuguese trailblazers in the 15th century sailed around Africa's coast all the way to India. What were they looking for?

Chapter 4

The Hugest "Discovery" 16

A mission from Spain in 1492 altered the world map beyond all recognition.

Chapter 5

Dead Ends 21

English explorers in Tudor times found it hard to sail through icy northern seas – but they had better luck further south.

Chapter 6

The Great Southern Mystery 24

Epic 18th-century voyages from Britain charted many lands in the Pacific Ocean but ended in disaster.

Chapter 7

To the Ends of the Earth 28

The world finally came into focus, thanks to awesome adventurers.

Maps 30

Glossary and Index 32

Chapter 1

What's Over the Horizon?

The Brits sound like a strange bunch!

For thousands of years, most of the world's people stayed quite close to home. They had little reason to travel and often did not know what lay over the horizon. Some let their imaginations go crazy ...

Fearing the Unknown

Imagine this scene nearly 2000 years ago. The mighty Roman army stands in wait on the northern shore of the country we now call France. The army is made up of 40 000 highly trained soldiers. These soldiers have made the Roman **Empire** one of the biggest empires in history.

Now the Roman army faces a new mission – to cross the sea and conquer Britain. There's just one problem ...

Dear Caesar,
We've never crossed this sea before and we know it's treacherous. Just a few years ago, a Roman fleet sank and the survivors washed up in Britain. They came back with terrifying tales of tornadoes, sea monsters and half-human creatures. We don't like the sound of that. We'd rather conquer a place less scary.
Yours,
Centurion Felix

Out of Touch

After several weeks of stalling, the Romans finally agreed to cross the sea. Nothing too scary happened to them; they conquered and then ruled most of Britain for 400 years. You can see how mysterious and frightening an unknown place could seem to even the bravest people.

For a long time, huge areas of the world remained a mystery. People didn't know how big the world was, what shape it was or what lay over the horizon. Many maps were drawn but often relied on guesswork rather than facts.

For thousands of years, Europeans had almost no contact with people in America and none at all with people in **Oceania**. Even within Europe itself, traders were really the only people to travel between countries.

Water Works Best

Traders often made their journeys by sea or river rather than overland. This map shows Europe, Western Asia and Northern Africa not long after the Romans conquered Britain.

■ Lands belonging to the Roman Empire

The busiest trading area was the inland Mediterranean Sea. Traders criss-crossed the sea in small, wide boats that could be rowed or sailed.

In contrast, most roads in history had terrible surfaces – and until the 1800s wheeled vehicles could only go as fast as the horses pulling them!

Branching Out

A few fully adventurous types in ancient times sailed west through the Mediterranean Sea and into the Atlantic Ocean. But it wasn't until the 1400s that it became more common to be adventurous and start to cross the vast oceans and discover new lands.

These adventures were incredibly long; land would not be sighted for months at a time. The vessels that were used were not much bigger than the ancient boats traders used to cross the Mediterranean Sea!

Aiming to Find Paradise

Trailblazers did not only set sail from Europe. People in the Middle East, China, India and Oceania made great voyages of exploration, too. But we're going to focus on Europe's trailblazers. So why did they set out to sea? Were they just curious about what lay beyond the horizon? Well – sort of. But that's not the whole story.

Remember the Romans who conquered Britain? They didn't just do this out of curiosity – they wanted Britain's wealth. Later, many seafarers had similar plans. Some wanted to trade goods, while others went in search of better places to live. And some others actually thought **Paradise** was somewhere across the seas!

As you will see, most of the trailblazers who mapped the world had more than one reason for exploring.

The Five Ms: An Explorer's Guide

Before you strike out into the unknown, you need:

- **Motive:** *a reason to leave the comfort of your own homeland and risk your life at sea*
- **Means:** *suitable ships, reliable maps and navigation skills*
- **Missionary zeal:** *a fierce religious faith that you can pass on to people in faraway lands*
- **Madness:** *because you have to be a bit mad to go on such daring adventures!*
- **"Me" factor:** *a desire to win fame and respect.*

What About the Locals?

It's one thing to feel the urge to "discover" new lands, but what about the people already living there? How did they feel about being "discovered"? Well, not great a lot of the time. Exploration didn't always benefit everyone.

The biggest boom in exploration happened after 1400, as you will see later on. However, one bunch of Europeans got out and about several centuries earlier – much to the dismay of the people they visited.

Whatever names you call us, we're still moving in.

Chapter 2

Vessels of the Vikings

About 1000-1200 years ago

The Romans were not the only people to invade Britain. From the 5th century on, **Angles** and **Saxons** arrived from Northern Europe. Then, three centuries later, fearsome Vikings from even further north began to land in Britain.

Fire-worshippers and Pirates!

From the 8th to the 11th century, Europe's most adventurous seafarers came from Norway, Sweden and Denmark. They weren't the best-behaved visitors and were given nicknames. In Ireland they were called "devils", in Spain "fire-worshippers" and in Britain "Vikings" – a word that may have meant "pirates".

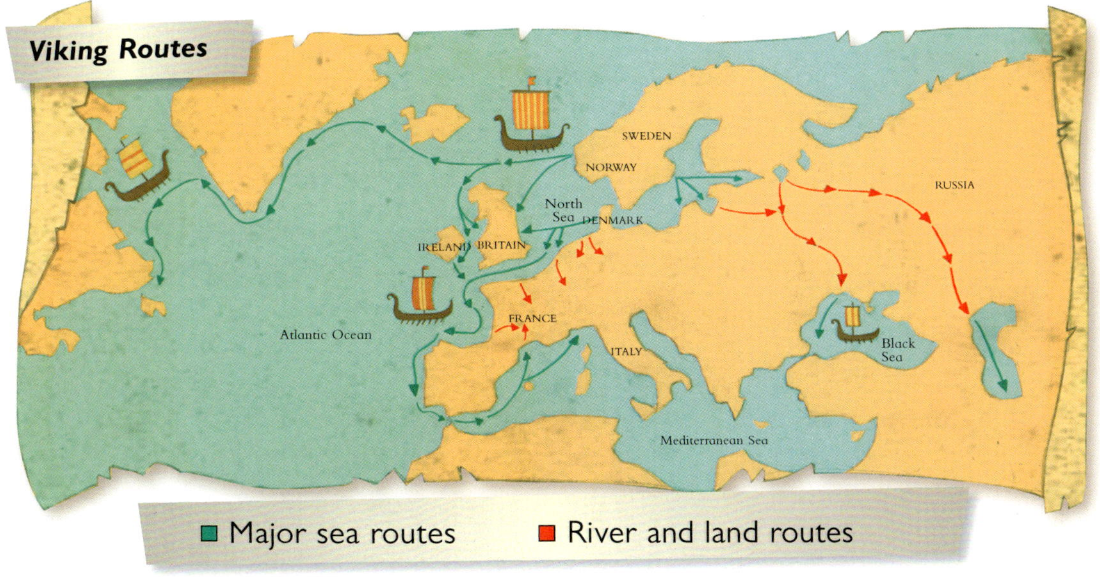

Calling All Vikings

A chance in a lifetime to set sail and:

- go raiding for treasure, especially from rich Christian churches and **monasteries**. (Please note: killing and burning down buildings is expected.)
- find better farmland for you and your family
- trade your furs and walrus ivory for other goods.

"In the Twinkling of an Eye"

Love them or not, there was no escaping the Vikings. They didn't just travel far, they travelled fast – thanks to their longships. Around 17.5 metres long and 2.5 metres wide, these longships could sail through bad storms and were shallow enough to sail up rivers. They were also light enough to be carried! No wonder a man called Photios from Eastern Europe said they would appear "suddenly, in the twinkling of an eye, like a wave of the sea, pouring over our frontiers".

This is an **Anglo-Saxon** image of a Viking ship – the house on board is probably an exaggeration, though!

America Ahoy!

What was it like to be at sea in a longship? The Vikings did not leave many accounts of their adventures, but a **contemporary** Anglo-Saxon poem about a Viking seafarer survives. Here is a translated verse:

> **The waves were often wild when I took my turn at the night-watch. I stood at the prow of the ship, my feet frozen with frost, while the ship tossed near the rocks. Hail swirled around me. I heard nothing but the sea booming ...**

Without these trailblazers, the oceans would never have been crossed by Europeans – the Vikings crossed the Atlantic Ocean. **Archaeologists** have found signs of a Viking camp in Canada. Stories suggest the Vikings were heading for Greenland but were blown off course to Newfoundland in Canada.

Nearly 500 years would pass before other Europeans landed on the North American continent. In the meantime, people in Europe weren't even aware that there was another huge continent to the west. If they had dreamed of voyaging abroad, it was to the south or the east.

Chapter 3

Spice Boys!

About 500 years ago

Medieval Portuguese sailors led the way in exploring the coastline of Africa. But, until 1488, no European had achieved the dangerous feat of sailing around Africa's **treacherous** southern tip. Why would anyone risk their life trying? The answer lay partly in rotten meat!

The Lure of the Indies

Wealthy medieval Europeans loved nothing more than eating some tasty meat, but once an animal was slaughtered, it was hard to stop the meat going "off". One way to **preserve** it was to use spices. And spices only came from the Far East, in the area we now call Asia: pepper from India, cinnamon from Sri Lanka, and cloves and nutmeg from the Maluku (Spice) Islands. In medieval times, these places were called "the Indies".

Spices were also in demand as medicines, dyes, perfumes and cosmetics. These spices – along with other luxury goods like silk from China – were brought overland across Asia and into Europe.

What did all that have to do with trailblazing sea voyages? In July 1497, people didn't give interviews but if they had, this is the story one Portuguese seafarer might have told.

Travel News: *We're here in sunny Portugal with Captain Vasco da Gama on the eve of his voyage. Captain da Gama, you're about to lead a trailblazing expedition all the way to the Indies – by sea! Has this ever been done before?*

Da Gama: *Not quite! Ten years ago my fellow-Portuguese captain, Bartholomew Dias, led an expedition around the southern tip of Africa into the Indian Ocean. But his men panicked in the stormy seas, fearing their food would run out, so he was forced to turn back. That will not happen under my command.*

Travel News: *But we hear you won't see land for three months!*

Da Gama: *Even without land in sight, my amazing* ***navigation*** *skills will keep us on track.*

Travel News: *What do you expect to find in the Indies?*

Da Gama: *Two things – spices and Christians.*

Travel News: *Pardon?*

Da Gama: *Spices – pepper, cloves and so on. The cost of transporting them overland is too high now, and sometimes the goods never arrive because routes are blocked and hostile rulers steal them. But if we open up a sea route, we'll ensure a cheaper, regular supply of luxury goods – while making a handsome profit ourselves. Hurrah!*

Travel News: *You said you expect to find Christians, too?*

Da Gama: *Indeed. We intend to find an eastern kingdom where there is no crime and no war, ruled by a Christian monarch named Prester John.*

Travel News: *Wow.*

Da Gama: *We've heard many rumours of this amazing kingdom. Our king, who is paying for this voyage, wants to make contact and unite the world's Christians. We can then convert the whole world to our glorious faith!*

Travel News: *Well, good luck with that – and with the weather. How long will the voyage take?*

Da Gama: *Dias was gone for over 16 months without reaching the Indies. I estimate two years for the round trip. It will be time, and money, well spent!*

Exotic Figures

Prester John was one of many exotic foreign figures that Europeans believed existed. A bestselling medieval book, *Travels of Sir John Mandeville*, described an Asian island where "the folk have only one foot, which is so broad it will cover all the body and shade it from the sun"!

A Portuguese Trading Empire

Vasco Da Gama did complete his 1497 voyage in just over two years (although half his crew lost their lives). He helped set up Portuguese trading posts in the Indies, and large amounts of spices and other luxury goods were shipped back to Europe.

Some people in the Indies didn't welcome these Portuguese seafarers and traders. But there was little they could do – they were up against the firepower of European naval guns.

Did Da Gama ever find Prester John? No, but this didn't stop many Europeans continuing to believe. Was Prester John ever found? Wait and see!

Thanks to men like Dias and Da Gama, Europeans learned about Africa and Asia. But other continents still remained unmapped!

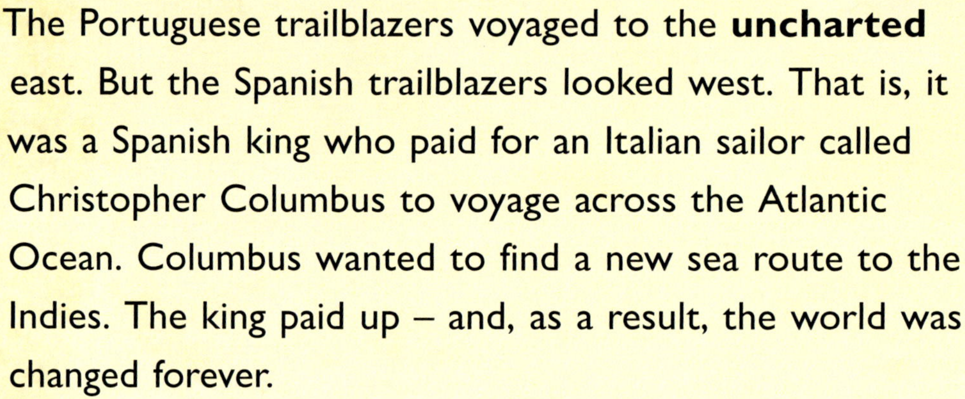

Chapter 4

The Hugest "Discovery"

About 500 years ago

The Portuguese trailblazers voyaged to the **uncharted** east. But the Spanish trailblazers looked west. That is, it was a Spanish king who paid for an Italian sailor called Christopher Columbus to voyage across the Atlantic Ocean. Columbus wanted to find a new sea route to the Indies. The king paid up – and, as a result, the world was changed forever.

Shortcut to the East

Columbus worked out that because the Earth was round, there was nothing to stop him reaching the Indies by sailing west from Europe. He calculated that the east of Asia was 3840 kilometres away and he thought it would only take 20 days to sail there.

Mystery Trip

Columbus set out in 1492 from the Canary Islands (on the north-west coast of Africa) with three ships. After more than 30 days into the voyage there was still no sign of land, and the crew began to worry. Columbus tried to keep them calm, but he soon realised the world was much larger than anyone thought.

Then, land finally appeared – the Indies! They anchored the three ships at some islands. Beyond them lay a longer coastline, thought to be the eastern edge of Asia. Columbus made a thorough **reconnaissance** of the region and was back in Spain six months later to report his findings.

Voyage West to the Indies: Mission Debrief

It will delight your majesty to learn that the voyage undertaken in your name proved to be a great success. The Indies were reached by sailing west – and now that contact has been made, you can trade with the people that live there.

It will interest you to know that we found gold, too – although the people there seem to hold it of little value. They are ***docile*** *people– wearing few clothes, owning few weapons, eager to please and quick to obey instructions given to them in sign language. Some are so uncivilised that they practise* ***cannibalism****! But once trained, they should make excellent servants. I believe they will also be easy to convert to our religion.*

They are indeed so childlike, there seems no reason why you should not seize their lands and rule them! It is recommended that a second voyage be made, to hurry the setting up of a glorious new Spanish Empire in the Indies.

Christopher Columbus

Ambushed by a Continent

Columbus made three more voyages. He explored more land in the west and claimed it for Spain. When he died in 1506, he still believed he'd reached the Indies (Asia). But he was wrong. The lands he found were islands in the Caribbean Sea – the Bahamas and Jamaica. The longer coastline he saw was Cuba. What he had found, quite by accident, was America.

Columbus didn't realise this, and he never actually set foot on the American mainland. Oh, and by the way... America hadn't exactly been "lost" in the first place!

A New World

The westward-voyaging Spanish, after Columbus, soon realised his mistake. They called this surprise continent the 'New World'.

New World Stores

Roll up, roll up! These brand new luxury goods are just in from the New World – all for the very first time in Europe!

Be tempted by a tomato, tuck into some peanuts and potatoes, try a taste of turkey, chill with a cool chocolate drink made from **cacao**, *make a meal out of maize, tone up your health with tobacco**, *add some vigour with vanilla – and when you're done, hang loose in a hammock!*

*The people in the 1500s were wrong about this. Smoking tobacco turned out to be one of the most unhealthy things you could do.

On the Treasure Trail

The most sought-after new goods were precious metals, especially silver. These were found in abundance in Central and South America.

It was mainly the desire to get rich that led the Spanish to conquer (or kill) the people of the New World and turn their lands into Spanish **colonies**. Native Americans who were not killed were converted to Christianity and forced to work for their new European masters.

The Race to Make a Fortune

During this time, there was a lot of wealth to be gained, so the two major exploration nations of Europe (Spain and Portugal) agreed to keep the peace as they raced to conquer the world.

In the Treaty of Tordesillas of 1494, they drew an imaginary line around the world. It divided the world into two "zones": one for the Spanish Empire and the other for the Portuguese Empire.

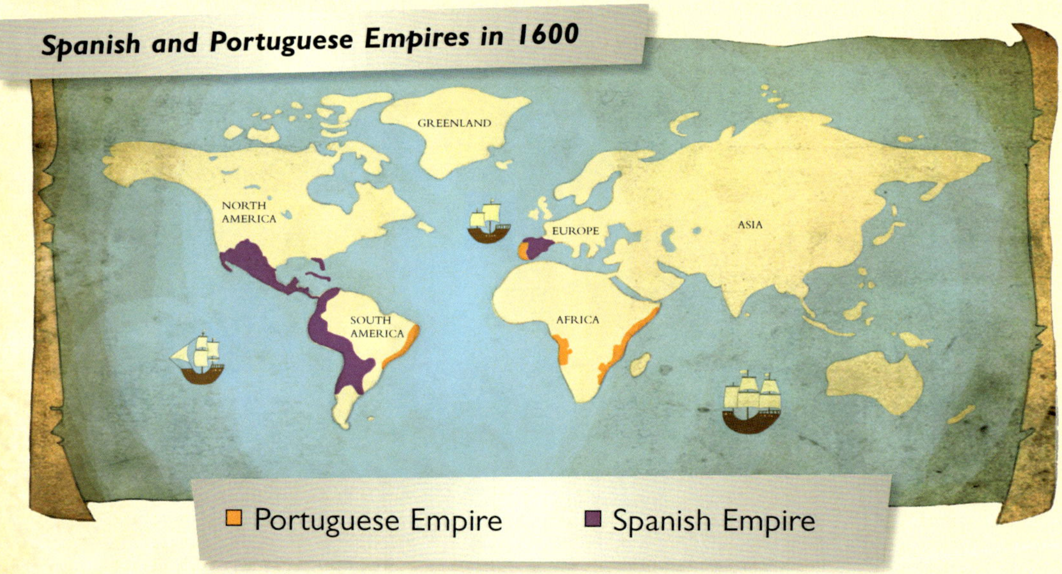

The treaty didn't go down well in other European countries like France, England and the Netherlands. Soon their rulers sent out explorers, too.

Brrr! This new route will be cool!

Chapter 5

Dead Ends

About 400 years ago

Despite the European explorers' modern ships and guns, and their maps and navigation skills, sailing into unknown places could still be very risky. Not every voyage went smoothly. Take a look at this picture of some Arctic explorers and their polar bear encounter!

An English Route to the Indies?

The **Tudor** monarchs of England were not as rich as the Spanish and Portuguese monarchs. Therefore, they were reluctant to pay for voyages of discovery for England. Fortunately, some wealthy English merchants were happy to pay because, like most businesspeople, they were on the lookout for new sales opportunities!

In 1553, eager to find a new route to the Indies (the real Indies, in Asia!), the English merchants paid for an expedition led by Sir Hugh Willoughby and Richard Chancellor.

It ended badly, though. Willoughby's ship got lost – and the crew perished in the freezing Arctic conditions. Chancellor sailed no further than Russia, and he drowned while returning to England.

In the mid-1570s, English captain Martin Frobisher made three attempts to find another route to the Indies, to the north of America. He failed all three attempts, but thanks to his voyages, more accurate maps of North America could be drawn.

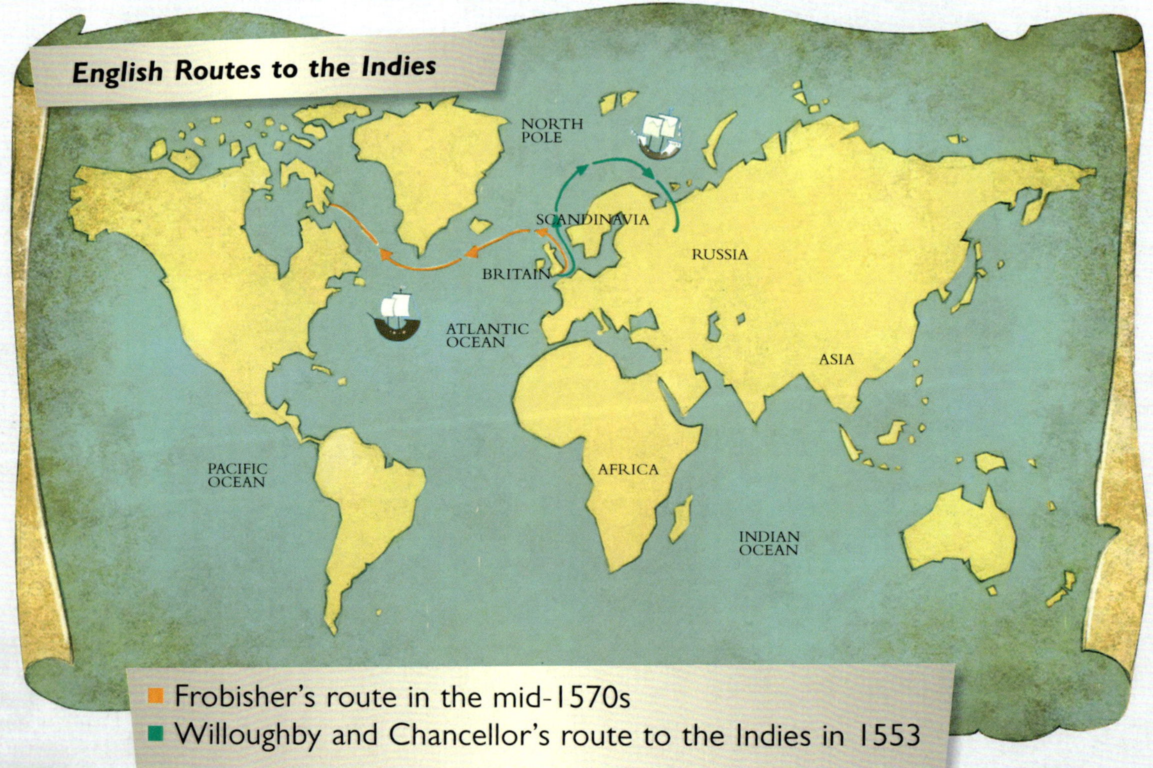

Another 300 years would pass before European explorers found east and west passages to the Indies across the north of the world. There were, however, some success stories from this age of exploration...

Around the World in 1000 Days (Plus)

At last it's been done! An incredibly brave and skilful seafarer has captained an expedition around the globe. Feisty Francis Drake is the world's first **circumnavigating** captain (try saying that into an ocean wind!) and the journey took him just under three years.

Drake hasn't just come back with lots of new info about the world. He also spotted a Spanish ship full of American silver and grabbed the lot to take back to England! No wonder Queen Elizabeth I has made him a knight! Good on you, Sir Frank!

But even Drake's expedition wasn't perfect. Part of his mission had been to find a new continent south of South America. Rumours had been circulating that a great southern land existed, but no one, including Drake, could find it.

Chapter 6

The Great Southern Mystery

About 250 years ago

Two centuries after Francis Drake's time, in the late 1700s, the great age of sailing ships was drawing to a close. But between 1768 and 1779, one man joined trailblazing seafarers such as the Vikings, Da Gama and Columbus. His name was James Cook, from northern England, and thanks to his three historic voyages, maps of the world began to be drawn correctly.

Sorting Out the South

People had always wondered what lands lay over the Equator in the southern half of the world. Seafarers were not as familiar with the Pacific Ocean either. It was much further away from Europe than the Atlantic Ocean, and seemed more mysterious.

Also, ancient Europeans believed the Equator could not be crossed – and those who tried would be burned to death! Later in history, some said there must be a great land mass in the south to "balance out" all the lands in the northern world. But no one knew if people could actually live there. Or was it – just maybe – that Paradise on Earth that some people believed in?

From Paradise to Polar Regions

In the 1600s, Dutch and British seafarers reached some islands in the southern part of the world and saw some others in the distance. But it was the brilliant navigator Captain James Cook who formed a clear picture of this vast region.

In 1768, the British Navy sent Cook into the Pacific on a fact-finding mission that lasted until 1770. He stopped at the island of Tahiti, then mapped the coasts of New Zealand and part of Australia. Soon, many lands in the south would become part of a growing British Empire, and would be changed forever.

On coming home, Cook was not sure if a great southern continent existed. So in 1772 he set off on a second expedition to investigate further.

Cook's ships headed south of Africa into the Southern Ocean. He and his crew encountered freezing temperatures as they sailed close to the Antarctic mainland.

Cook soon realised that no one could live in these harsh conditions. He sailed on to the much warmer Pacific Ocean where he mapped more than 30 previously unknown islands. Cook made his men treat the Pacific Islanders they met with greater respect than explorers had in the past. He also traded goods with them to get fresh food supplies.

1774, somewhere in the Pacific

Dear Mum, Dad and Spot,

We're now into the third year of this voyage and I'd normally be as sick as a dog by now, but not this time. No **scurvy** *for me – bleeding under the skin is a thing of the past. Cook, our captain, has solved that problem. He makes us eat healthy stuff like limes. And you know what? We hardly ever get sick now! He's a top bloke, our skipper. Not just a great navigator but a great nutritionist, too!*

Bye for now,

Edwin

P.S. I hope Spot has learned to sit now, Dad!

What Cook learned was that there were plenty of lands in the Pacific but no single great land mass. These lands – Australia, New Zealand, New Guinea and the Pacific Islands – all made up the area now known as Oceania.

However, the mysterious reputation of the south remained... Cook's men found these huge stone heads on Rapa Nui (Easter Island). Imagine their surprise when they stumbled across them!

End of the Great Adventure

In 1776, Cook made his third and final voyage. He sailed to New Zealand, Tahiti, the Hawaiian Islands, and then up the Pacific coast of North America. He was looking for a quick north-west passage, at the top of North America, back to Europe. He could not find this passage, so turned around. He stopped again at the Hawaiian Islands. Sadly, his crew and the Islanders fought and Captain Cook was killed.

So, you see, exploring the world was fully adventurous but also fully dangerous.

To the ends of the Earth ... and beyond!

Chapter 7

To the Ends of the Earth

Captain Cook once wrote that he wanted "to go as far as it is possible for man to go". And he went further than any other explorer of his time. Since the beginning of exploration, brave adventurers have mapped the lands and the seas; others have even studied Earth from the surface of the Moon. But it was because of the seafarers of the past that people first learned about what lay over the horizon.

In this old painting, a seafarer tells two boys about his adventures at sea. One of these boys would grow up to become a famous British explorer – Sir Walter Raleigh.

Thinking Big

European seafarers were fully adventurous! In ancient and medieval times, sailors began to venture far from home. Then, from the 1400s, exploration went global!

Europeans made up around 15 per cent of the world's population – but Europe's explorers liked to think BIG. Through their voyages they found out how large the world was and were able to map it accurately. But they didn't find a Paradise on Earth. Nor did they ever track down Prester John, although they kept on looking!

Not Always Good News

Exploration didn't always have a good outcome. When Europeans encountered **indigenous** people, there were some brutal clashes. The European explorers rarely treated the local inhabitants well and many suffered or died as a result.

But, whatever the rights or wrongs, you can't stop human beings – the fully adventurous ones – from wanting to go to the ends of the Earth and beyond! The stories of their amazing explorations will always take our breath away.

Maps

Here are the routes taken by the fully adventurous explorers we have looked at:

Viking Routes

- Major sea routes
- River and land routes

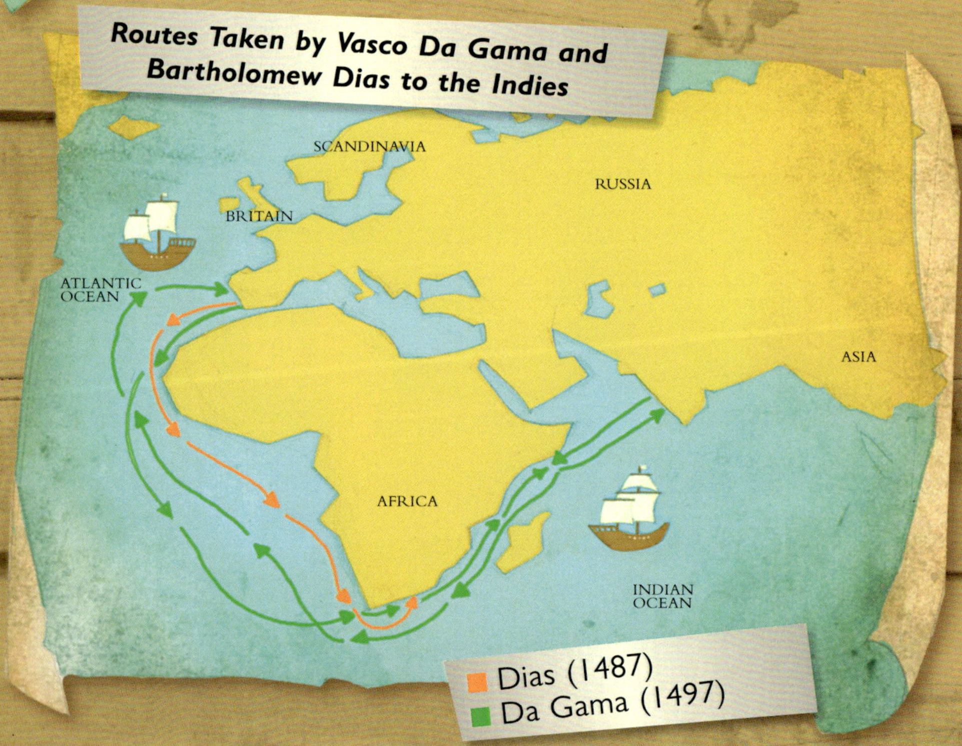

Routes Taken by Vasco Da Gama and Bartholomew Dias to the Indies

- Dias (1487)
- Da Gama (1497)

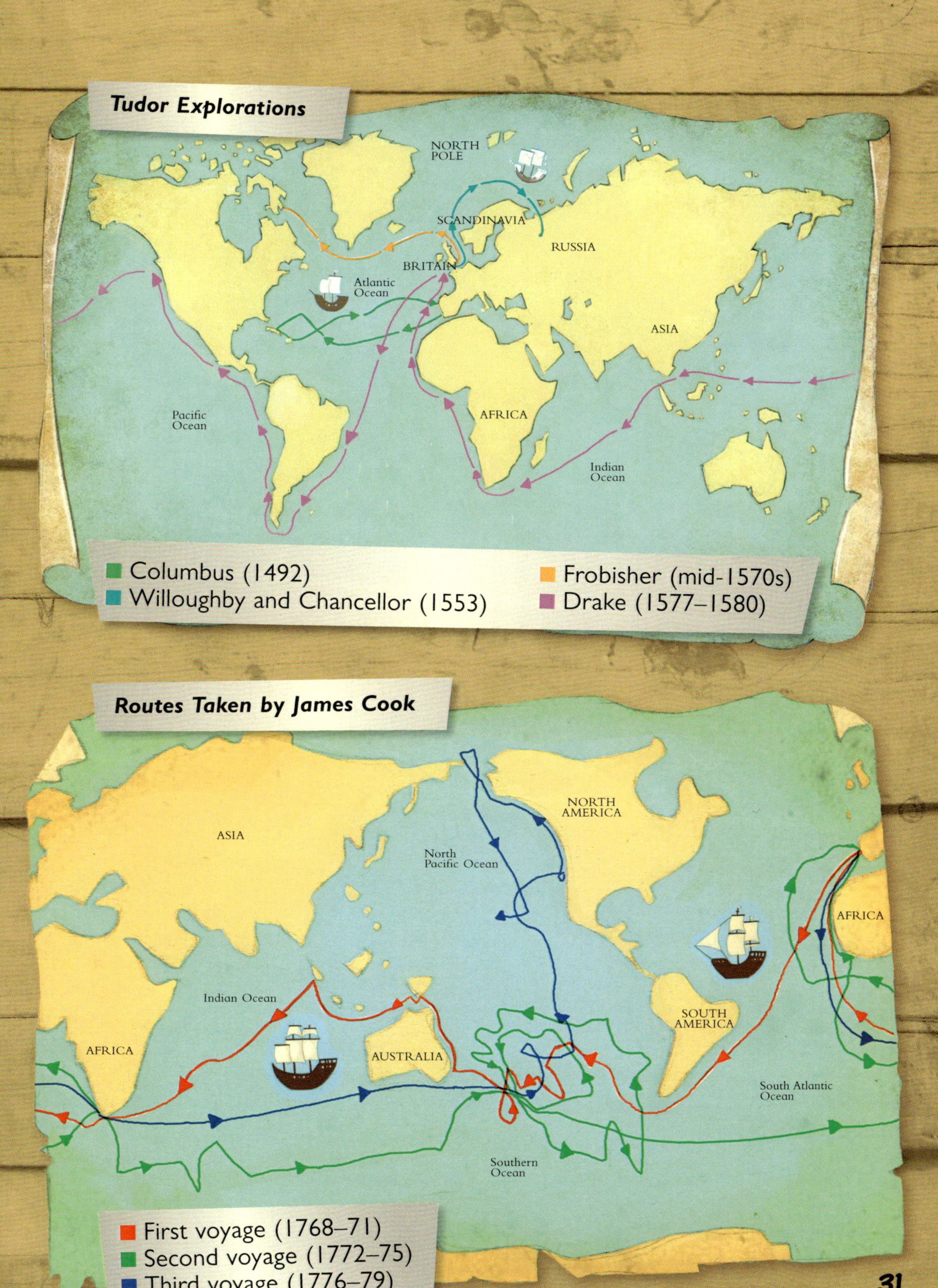

Tudor Explorations
NORTH POLE
SCANDINAVIA
RUSSIA
BRITAIN
Atlantic Ocean
ASIA
Pacific Ocean
AFRICA
Indian Ocean
Columbus (1492)
Willoughby and Chancellor (1553)
Frobisher (mid-1570s)
Drake (1577–1580)
Routes Taken by James Cook
ASIA
NORTH AMERICA
North Pacific Ocean
AFRICA
Indian Ocean
AFRICA
AUSTRALIA
SOUTH AMERICA
South Atlantic Ocean
Southern Ocean
First voyage (1768–71)
Second voyage (1772–75)
Third voyage (1776–79)

Glossary

Angles: people from an area around Germany who invaded England in the 5th century
Anglo-Saxon: name given to Germanic people who settle in England in the 5th and 6th centuries
archaeologists: people who study the past by digging up objects
cacao: large seed used to make chocolate and cocoa
cannibalism: practice of eating human flesh
circumnavigating: sailing around the world
colonies: places where groups of people come to settle which are under the control of their home country
contemporary: happened in the same period of time
docile: obedient and easy to manage
empire: group of nations under one ruler or government
indigenous: local or native
medieval: relating to the Middle Ages (around 400–1500 CE)
monasteries: buildings used by communities of monks
navigation: setting of a course for a ship to follow
Oceania: the south, west and central islands in the Pacific Ocean
Paradise: fictional kingdom, filled with riches and happiness
preserve: treat food so that it will last longer
prow: front part of a ship
reconnaissance: examining a place to gain useful information about that place
Saxons: people from northern Germany who invaded Britain in the 5th and 6th century
scurvy: a disease caused by a lack of vitamin C in the diet
treacherous: dangerous
Tudor: royal family that ruled England 1485–1603
uncharted: not recorded on any map or chart

Index

America 5, 11, 18–19, 27
circumnavigation 23
Columbus, Christopher 16–18
Cook, James 24–28
indigenous peoples 17, 19, 29
maps 5, 6, 21, 22, 24, 29, 30–31
Oceania 5, 27
Romans 4–5, 6, 7
spices 12–14, 15
trade 5, 6, 7, 10, 21
treasure 10, 17, 19, 20, 23
Vikings 9–11